MW00976819

Church Hurts
Hope for Hearts in Transition
By: Momentum Church Woodstock

Church Hurts
© 2019 Momentum Church Woodstock.
All rights reserved
ISBN: 978-0-359-64470-4

Church Hurts
Hope for Hearts in Transition

This book was collaboratively written by the following Pastors at Momentum Church:

Ross Wiseman: Lead Pastor

Amie Wiseman: Children's Pastor

Brantley Johnson: Executive Pastor

Corey Blair: Worship Pastor

Stephanie Robison: Connections Pastor

Table of Contents

INTRODUCTION

In 2005 our family moved to plant a church in a growing community. For several years we looked back over our shoulders at our home church and missed the community that once loved and embraced us. There were times we didn't know if we would ever experience what we felt in our last church.

Over time, the sense of belonging, ease of community and combined purpose began to develop. Soon we grew to have very similar feelings for those that we currently fellowship with as a church family. I believe that sense of belonging takes time to develop, but I also believe there are things that we can do and questions that can be answered that can help serve to make a new church feel more quickly like home. That is the goal of this guide.

I pray the chapters in this guide will help you during your season of transition.
You will not relate to every chapter, but use the Table of Contents to direct you to chapters that will serve your experience and current state of prayerful transition.

Transition looks different through the lens of every individual so we have included several contributors in the compilation of this guide. Let's begin by looking at several reasons people transition from one church to another. Each of these create issues and these issues will be addressed in the following chapters of this guide.

REASONS FOR TRANSITIONING TO A NEW CHURCH

Reason #1 New to the Area

Like our family's transition, maybe you have moved to a new area and it is not possible to remain an active part of your previous church. This can be a very painful part of moving. Recreating what you once experienced is not something that is difficult, it is something that is impossible.

There may be similarities in vision and purpose, music style and sermon delivery, but this community has not been created in a vacuum. This new church will be unique because it is flavored by the city it is planted in and is marked by the people that make up it's unique community. This community, if you feel called to be a part of, will be something that in time will mark you and be marked by you.

Be patient if you are in transition because of moving to a new area. Know that God has the right place for you even if it may feel in some ways different than home. Your new city feels strange to you, but that sense of belonging and familiarity we all crave is just a few relationships and experiences away.

Reason #2 I've Been Hurt

Often people look to transition on the backside of being hurt. It's been said that "No hurt hurts like Church Hurts". This may be a hurt that you received from church leadership. The pastor may have directly let you down. A ministry leader may have broke confidence and shared things that you felt diminished you in the community. A person in the church that you felt as close to as your own family began to lash out at you and the very place you felt should provide a sense of safety and rest now is a place of exhausting tension. Whatever the cause of the hurt often the solution is to try and find community elsewhere.

Reason #3 I Don't Feel Like I am Growing Anymore

There are seasons in our development as believers that it is necessary for us to experience growth that can only come from a different church experience. Every church is unique in what its focus is. That uniqueness may cause you over time to need a different flow of teaching or ministry opportunities that will stretch you.

I believe on one hand, that a long-term commitment to a church is best in order to see spiritual development. Sporadically attending various churches over a long period of time will greatly reduce your ability to be discipled and developed. On the other hand, I believe at times God will lead someone to be an active part of another congregation because He is desiring for them to grow in such a way that is not possible in one's current church community.

Reason #4 You Have it, I Want It

You have been in your church for a while and now you have different needs that your current church does not address. This may be related to seasons in your life. The ministry you have been a part of focused on young professionals and singles, but now you are married with children. You want a place that has more to offer your children than your current church. You are entering into your golden years, but the church you attend has nothing to offer senior saints. You're a man, but the greater percentage of the church is made up of women and you are looking for a place that you can be mutually challenged by other men. Or maybe you are a single person and it's seems like the church is made up mostly of marrieds with children. This different culture looks appealing and able to meet the needs that you have.

Reason #5 God is Leading You

You feel a need to transition to a new church and your awareness of this need is separate from any discontentment, hurt, or sense of reason for leaving. God may be positioning you for something that you just wouldn't be able to experience where you currently are attending.

We have a man in our church who felt led to come but absolutely loved his previous church. Upon coming to our church, over time, he became extremely influential in ministering to men. His impact has led to numerous men's groups and ministries that meet the spiritual needs of men. Our church and this man both benefited because he embraced the call of God on his life to leave a church that he loved to begin being a part of a church family in which he didn't even know one person.

This call to go can manifest different ways. God can place you in a new church for what you need next in your development. At times, He will also place people in a new church for what they can do to help others develop.

No matter what your reason is that has you thinking about transitioning to a new church, please pray. Make this a spiritual decision and not a decision rooted in hurt or just a desire to see if the grass is greener. If this is a decision born out of the heart of the Father you can be confident, even if the transition feels awkward at first, you will walk in the Father's blessing as you make this transition.

CHECKLIST FOR DETERMINING WHY I SHOULD STAY

☐ God has not released me from my current church.

☐ There is an area that the church lacks where I am gifted and equipped to make a difference.

☐ The hurt I experienced has not been attempted to be reconciled by myself. To leave without trying to reconcile would mean that I am running away from the growth God desires for me to have by facing this hurt.

☐ My desire to leave has more to do with my preferences than any principles being violated or neglected.

☐ I can get behind 80% of the ministry and decisions that have been made. *Know this....you will never be 100% in regards to your opinions about any organization. The Church is no different.*

☐ I am facing challenges in my current church. Ask yourself, is this tension I am experiencing something God wants me to lean into so that He might develop me through the frustration and tension?

CHECKLIST FOR DETERMINING WHY I SHOULD GO

☐ The Church is teaching false doctrine or excepting practices that are not Biblical.

☐ The Church does not put an emphasis on the Word of God.

☐ The Church is missing key areas of ministry that I or my family need to be discipled and has no plans to offer those areas in the future.

☐ The Church has no push to reach the lost and disciple them. Evangelism is a low priority.

☐ Leadership hasn't challenged and/or helped reconciliation to happen between myself and the person that has hurt me.

☐ I am currently living further than a 40 minute drive to the church. It is hard to be active in a church family if you live much further than 30 minutes from the church campus.

GETTING YOU WHOLE IS MORE IMPORTANT THAN GETTING YOU HERE

One morning in the office I heard my administrator laughing in the other room. She had just got off the phone with someone inquiring about getting married at the church. My admin explained to her that I would be willing to marry them, but that they would need to commit to 4-5 pre-marital counseling sessions. The woman inquiring proceeded to say, "we've both been married several times each we don't need any pre-marital counseling. We just want to know how much it will cost to get the preacher to marry us". Obviously, my admin explained that the counseling was for their benefit and that I wouldn't be willing to marry them if they wouldn't do the counseling. She also let her know it wasn't about a money, but it is about our commitment to help them have a good foundation to start on. The woman made it clear that they would just look elsewhere.

My job as a pastor is to represent Jesus and His style of leadership, care and concern regarding people. Scripture teaches us that Jesus is the Great Shepherd who leads us in the way we should go. He does this for our benefit.

Psalm 23:1-3

1 The Lord is my shepherd; I shall not want. 2 He makes me lie down in green pastures. He leads me beside still waters. 3 He restores my soul. He leads me in paths of righteousness for his name's sake.

There are times when the Great Shepherd is leading a person or family to be a part of a new church home. This may well be what is going on in your life. This can be a difficult time as God leads you into what is next for you. The loving team at the new church you are exploring can help you during your transition. Like shepherds leading you to good pasture they are there to guide you. You are not a number. You are a precious lamb of God and He has a place prepared for you that will help you grow and become strong and healthy in Him.

When meeting guests at church for the first time, I am always excited and honored that they have visited the church. I know that if God is leading them to our church body that He has a plan to bless them and for them to be a blessing.

I get to be their pastor (shepherd). What an incredible sacred trust and responsibility to receive. I embrace it fully and look forward to the years to come of journeying with them through good times and bad as we watch them grow as followers of The Great Shepherd.

There are other times when meeting guests, they will say something that makes it clear they are leaving a church for a specific reason.

... "Those people did me wrong"
... "That church is just too judgmental"
... "I just can't grow under that pastor anymore"

Often people make a church transition because of a hurt, a brokenness, or a refusal to receive what God is trying to do in their life in the ministry that they are leaving. Things guests say at times makes me feel like God just might not be through with them yet at the church they are leaving.

Remember what I said, as a pastor it is my job to serve the Great Shepherd, to lead people to a place of wholeness. It is not my job just to take your money and begin working for you. The lady talking to my admin who just wanted to pay for services rendered so that she could get married asked the question, "How much does it cost". Well it will cost you a great deal if a pastor isn't concerned about leading you as a shepherd but is just excited to count you as a number in the flock. It will cost you a great deal of growth and maturity if God isn't through with you under the leadership of the ministry you are leaving.

I want you to hear this clearly...

Getting you whole is more important than getting you here.

Of course, I want our church to grow. Of course, you would be a wonderful person and family to have, but at whose benefit?

If you are leaving because of a hurt, it just might be that God wants you to stay where you are coming from because He is going to develop in you the Fruit of the Spirit in the area of patience. He is going to teach you, if pursued, the power of reconciliation.

Maybe something in you is being challenged by the teachings and culture of the church you are leaving, but it is you that needs to change, not them. Maybe you aren't growing under the leadership of the church you are running from because you won't receive what they are saying. If this is the case, it's not a new church that you need, it's a new heart. A renewed heart. A heart set on becoming whole again. I want you here, but I want you whole even more.

The woman who was ready to begin a new exciting time on her third marriage, with no thought that she needed counsel, speaks to me concerning this. Most likely there are areas of growth that she needs to develop in that are being missed by not hanging in the relationship. Something new always seems exciting and fresh. The problem in chasing the new means the pain left behind isn't being dealt with. The growth that is possible is forfeited for a new church honeymoon high.

In the early days of the Church you had THE Church of Corinth, THE Church of Ephesus, THE Church at Rome. If you were under church discipline, there wasn't the ability to just go down the street and start over with a new group of people. You had to face correction and embrace repentance. In doing so, you would experience wholeness through God's forgiveness and leadership regarding how He would have you to live.

If you were at odds with someone, neither party could take their ball and just go to another court. No, you were at THE Church in town and y'all were just going to have to work it out. Again, this led to wholeness rather than a temporary fix. To not try to be reconciled will only hurt you deeper in the end.

Yes, there are times when relationships are toxic and stepping away is necessary. There are times when the ministry of a church isn't healthy and they have relinquished their right to lead you to good pasture. There are times when you need a new church and a new shepherd to lead you to what God has next for you to make you whole. We want you here, but we want you whole even more. If here is where God will make you whole, we can't wait to be a part of that. If going back to where you are coming from is what you need, we care more about the foundation you are building for life than we do just marrying you to a new church family. Our prayers are with you as you seek God during this transition.

WHY CHURCH IS IMPORTANT

Something happens that's different. It's different in a larger group environment than it is at home. Here's the thing: We all are tempted with very good reason to stay home.

For the longest time, I thought it was a stupid argument that I needed to be in church. Nobody had given me any kind of logical/Biblically incredible argument that the Church was very necessary. However, as I read, pray and study, I find that there are actually a few different reasons it is important for me to be in a church. It is a marrying of sorts that is between our personal pursuit and that of the church. Sure, you can watch your favorite preacher online. You can listen to your favorite worship songs in the order that you would choose.

It benefits you to do that.

Absolutely.

No sarcasm.

It benefits you to actively pursue new teachings and embrace a lifestyle that is constantly worshipping and singing the praises to the King. It's all good. It benefits you to read your Bible in the quietness of your home and pray in silence.

Because He is in those moments.

Scripture makes reference to His "still small voice" and those are the times it is most often and easiest to hear that voice.

It's harder to find those kinds of moments in a large room, filled with people who are shouting, singing and dancing before a King who is worthy of crowds larger than we could imagine, let alone produce.

But it seems more logical and better for you to be at home in the still, small moments with God.

People can't hurt you there anyway.

Right?

Well, I understand the temptation. You don't even have to get out of your jammies...or your bed. While I certainly see all of the benefits of staying at home, would it be okay if I painted a bit of a picture for you?

Let's start with some scripture and as we read through, please feel free to explore the whole of scripture to find that this example and explanation are well represented and supported throughout scripture.

Going into Nehemiah 4 the walls of Jerusalem had been burned down and the city lay in ruins. Nehemiah had gathered people together to start the rebuild process and now kings from the surrounding cities had taken issue with them rebuilding and as such began threatening them to stop.

(Insert war music here)

Nehemiah 4:14-20 [NASB]
14 After I looked things over, I stood up and said to the nobles, the officials and the rest of the people, "Don't be afraid of them. Remember the Lord, who is great and awesome, and fight for your families, your sons and your daughters, your wives and your homes." 15 When our enemies heard that we were aware of their plot and that God had frustrated it, we all returned to the wall, each to our own work. 16 From that day on, half of my men did the work, while the other half were equipped with spears, shields, bows and armor. The officers posted themselves behind all the people of Judah 17 who were building the wall.

Those who carried materials did their work with one hand and held a weapon in the other, 18 and each of the builders wore his sword at his side as he worked. But the man who sounded the trumpet stayed with me.
19 Then I said to the nobles, the officials and the rest of the people, "The work is extensive and spread out, and we are widely separated from each other along the wall. 20 Wherever you hear the sound of the trumpet, join us there. Our God will fight for us!"

This is the essence of our individual pursuits with God and our congregational pursuits with God. Everyone had the individual responsibility to work and be prepared for battle. However, together, their individual responsibilities translated into them working together to build the kingdom and to fight for each other. The work was extensive and at times, they were separated far from each other. However, when the trumpet blew, it was time for them to come together to fight.

This is the healthy work. It is the combination of individual efforts combined with the church that produces positive results for the Kingdom of God to which we have all been called. It is the combined effort that leads to us furthering the kingdom through worshipping and laboring selflessly as well as leading us into a community that fights for each other on both the spiritual and physical realms.

You have a call not just to rebuild your house but also to rebuild the walls.

At some point, the realization will strike you that we have to be in this thing together. We have work to do and battles to fight. When we fight alone, we fight weakly. Together, we are stronger. Together we can achieve more.

If you understand this principle and your purpose, then you also can understand that sometimes injuries happen in war. As we look at engaging in a spiritual war with the enemy, he would love for you to get in the way of one of your companions. If he can work you in between a blow that was intended for the enemy, then you will be hurt instead of his army. That's what happens.

We accidentally get in the way.

Through poor choices by us or by others, we get hurt.

We have to fully grasp that there are only two sides to this battle. The enemy and the Church. As hard as you may try, you cannot create a third side.

It doesn't exist.

Therefore, if you are with the Church, you stand back up, shake off the hurt and get back to the fight.

Not just for you.

Not just for your family.

But for the Kingdom.

20 Wherever you hear the sound of the trumpet, JOIN US THERE. Our God will fight for us!"

NO HURT LIKE CHURCH HURT

This chapter may sting a bit. You've made it this far, so I can only assume you are stronger than most. Nonetheless, I would like for you to pray before continuing. Just ask God to open your eyes to the things you may not want to see.

Here we go.

One of the number one reasons I hear for people not attending church is, "I was hurt by church." I'm sure there are some crazy, extreme cases where the entirety of a church cast someone out, but that is not what most people experience. Most people experience a bad situation with a handful or less of people.

Here's the thing, even if you had a bad experience with the lead pastor at your former church, it still was not that church that you were hurt by. You were hurt by someone or some people.

I'm going to say it one more time, a little bit clearer:

You were not hurt by the church, you were hurt by people in the church.

This is hard for most people to accept or at least adopt completely. We don't like having the feeling that a person here or there can have that much power over us. We feel like that looks weak in the eyes of the people around us that we expertly tell our story to. So, we decide to shift blame to something that is clearly larger than us in an effort to justify our flight path to those people who are partially engaged in our lives.

By attacking the church, it removes responsibility for repair off of us in the situation and puts it on the organization.

Can we agree for a minute that no church, church leadership or any congregant is perfect? Can we also agree that all have sinned and fallen short of the glory of God? In fact, I would venture to say that at minimum, if someone at your church doesn't frustrate you at some point, you are not living life close enough to anyone in your church.

If you are going to be able to heal and move successfully past what you consider "church hurt," you will have to deal with two things: Identifying and Repairing.

If you remember in the last chapter, towards the end, I stated there is no third side. You must identify which side you are on, because in identifying your side or your team, you also identify the purpose with which that team works to win. In uniting with your team/purpose you are fully aware that both you and your teammates at times will make mistakes. However, you are all committed to working towards victory.
With that in mind, you are not on a team that is merely a handful of people. You are a part of a much larger team. At times that may mean that you shift away from some teammates in order for the team to see victory. At times though, it means fixing the mistake and moving forward together.

Remember, there are only two teams. You cannot create a third.

The second part to moving forward is repairing. This is the part no one wants to talk about because we tend to have an all or nothing kind of mentality. Is it possible to accept that repair can happen even if we plan on never engaging with someone or some people again?

We all like bridge analogies, right? You cross over one day on a bridge that is broken and unstable. Whew! You made it. That may be a bridge you have to cross consistently and therefore, it needs to be repaired.

On the other hand, it may be a bridge that has been repaired many times and you are never quite able to trust it. You plan to never come back by that way, but because you don't know what tomorrow will bring, you decide it is probably best to repair the bridge rather than burn it.

In that example, Lord willing, you never have to go that way again. But, for the benefit of yourself and your team, it is more beneficial to repair the bridge in case you or someone else on your team has to cross it.

More times than not, you will need to be able to repair relationships because you don't need to leave. You just need to have a good conversation and work through the mistakes. If you feel like it is best to put space between you and the person/people that hurt you, a conversation to reconcile still needs to take place.

I think it is probably a critical piece to include here, that just because you leave, does not mean you are healed or can heal properly. Merely covering a wound, does not mean it will heal. Putting up large walls is not an example of healthy boundaries but is actually a better example of slow isolation. Which, by the way, is exactly what the enemy wants for your life.

If you are committed to the team, you are committed to repairing the mistakes.

Here's what it looks like:

1. Pray that God would open the situation and prepare it for healing.

2. Don't walk in with the expectation that you will leave either best friends or worst enemies.

3. Be honest with yourself and others involved about the part you played in the hurt. It will be nearly impossible for you to repair anything when you are not honest about the repair work that actually needs to be done on your end also.

4. Ask for forgiveness for the part you played in the turmoil.

5. Express how you felt or how the person/people made you feel.

6. If they apologize to you, forgive them openly. If they don't apologize, forgive them privately and ask God to help mend your heart.

7. Learn from the situation and move forward appropriately. (This does not mean lighting them up openly or passively on social media. Be a Christian. After all, you are representing our team.)

LEARNING TO TRUST AGAIN

Someone once said, "Trust takes years to build, seconds to break, and forever to repair". As sad as it is, for most of us, that's the reality we live in. From the early years of "Stranger Danger" to the later years of soured relationships and broken promises, we grow into a place of polite distrust. We smile and nod when people grace us with advice that we have no intention of heeding. We avoid at all cost those relationships that we just don't have the energy to invest in in order to get to a place of trust.

As perfect as we all wish pastors and church people were, there are times when we find ourselves on the short end of the trust stick. Perhaps a fellow church attender took advantage of your confidence. Maybe a Pastor used you for your talent in service and never expressed appreciation leaving you feeling used. Whatever your past hurt might be, we all have ample opportunity to offend, and sometimes even us Christians make the wrong decisions and hurt people around us.

This is not the end. In order to allow ourselves to explore the vulnerability of trust once again, we first need to have a clear understanding of its proper place.

Where Trust Belongs

My three sons LOVE swimming! If they had their way, every vacation would be spent at a pool, in the water, period! This wasn't always the case. The smallest of the three has always had a bit of a timid nature. Our first several outings to pools consisted of him having an absolute choke hold on whatever poor adult was willing to get in the water. Eventually we got him a little life jacket to wear but trust it he did not. Still like a Koala on a tree, he clung for life to the nearest sturdy object.

It took some convincing, but eventually he would float just holding my arm. Then he settled for my hand. After some time, he could go in the water alone but stay very near the edge. Eventually, confidence grew and he ventured out to the deep and joined his brothers. None of this would have ever been possible had I not been there to calm him and speak the confidence needed into him. His trust was not in the water nor the life jacket. It was in the security that his father loves him and would not let harm come to him.

To this day he is still cautious around water; but even when, not if, water goes up his nose, or he loses breath below the surface, or the depths get too deep, he knows that, if he keeps his father within his line of sight, he's going to be okay.

In Matthew 14, we find Jesus coming to his Disciples during a storm. Terrified and unsure, Peter tests Jesus by having him beckon him to come out on the water...

29 And He said, "Come!" And Peter got out of the boat and walked on the water and came toward Jesus. 30 But seeing the wind, he became frightened, and beginning to sink, he cried out, "Lord, save me!" 31 Immediately Jesus stretched out His hand and took hold of him, and *said to him, "You of little faith, why did you doubt?" 32 When they got into the boat, the wind stopped. 33 And those who were in the boat worshiped Him, saying, "You are certainly God's Son!"

As long as we keep Christ in our line of sight and our trust in Him, not even standing in the middle of the deepest lake of doubt during the worst storms of life, will He allow us to be overwhelmed. Trust that God has called you to community and walk in that calling (Hebrews 10:24-25). Trust that he has work for you to accomplish within and alongside that community (1 Peter 4:8-11, Ephesians 2:10).

Our world is a temporary and flawed place. Everything will eventually fail you. Pastors, friends, finances, cars, even your very body will fail at some point. If our trust is placed in any of those things, we are setting ourselves up for disappointment. Trust the Father.

Proverbs 3:5 Trust in the Lord with all your heart and do not lean on your own understanding. 6 In all your ways acknowledge Him, And He will make your paths straight.

If you're having trouble with learning to trust again, I would advise following the example of my son... With Christ being the Father, the Church being the life jacket, and the general pitfalls of life being the water.
It all starts with clinging to the father! If you're not there, what are you waiting for? Allow the Father to use the Church as a tool to help you float when you can't swim on your own. That's the whole purpose of the Church, to lift one another up and

encourage us in relationship with the Father to keep swimming.

As your confidence grows you can join a small group and put a little more faith in those around you (still grasping the father's arm). Next you can start serving in a ministry and get to know those around you better as you join together with a common mission. Before you know it, you and the Church are one, still in the protective sight of the Father. You can do this!

I would like to leave you with a blessing from Romans 15:13.

"May the God of hope fill you with all joy and peace as you trust in him, so that you may overflow with hope by the power of the Holy Spirit."

NO CHURCH IS A ONE STOP SHOP

I love malls! All under one roof you can get clothes, dishes, a new iPad, and your haircut. It's a one stop shop all designed to give me, the consumer, anything I want. For years the church has tried be a spiritual version of a mall. If you think you need it, then we have to have it. If we don't have it, you'll just go down the street to a church that does. This mall mentality has failed the church and has encouraged a consumer driven Christianity.

In the late 90's when Mall Church was all the rage, I was on staff at a church that celebrated having over 100 ministries. The problem that I saw was that we had a 100 ministries pulling on the resources of people and finances. To be honest we had about a dozen ministries that were good. The other 90 were things pulling on the resources that kept those dozen ministries from becoming great. Why did we try to do so much? Because it's what the consumer....I mean new person coming to church said they needed and wanted.

This pursuit of trying to be a one stop shop is futile. There will be as many things to start and try to maintain as there are people attending your church. Frankly, every one of us wants our every need and interest met now. So, we start a knitting ministry, after school program, boys club, hunting fellowship, food pantry, dance team, intercessory prayer and deliverance ministry, financial counseling ministry, coffee shop, second hand store, mission trips, Sunday school, small groups, choir, kids' choir and on it on it goes.

There is nothing wrong with all the things you see above. The list in most churches is beyond what it can do well. I don't believe it is God leading us to have a long list of ministries to meet the needs of people. I believe it is our consumer mentality that has caused church leadership try to accommodate everyone so that they will stay at our church.

The problem is the list given to the church was actually pretty short. Preach the gospel. Baptize those who receive the gospel. Make Disciples. Take care of the widows and orphans. Obviously, there are ministries needed in the church that meet the needs of people and facilitate these larger mandates we are called to do. In the list above, we have some of those ministries at our church and even other ones that aren't listed. I am not saying a church shouldn't have a good balance of ministry to make a difference in people's lives. I am just saying that no one church can have every ministry or preference represented under one roof. Thank God we don't have to.

1 Corinthians 12:12-27 (ESV)

12 For just as the body is one and has many members, and all the members of the body, though many, are one body, so it is with Christ. 13 For in one Spirit we were all baptized into one body—Jews or Greeks, slaves or free—and all were made to drink of one Spirit. 14 For the body does not consist of one member but of many. 15 If the foot should say, "Because I am not a hand, I do not belong to the body," that would not make it any less a part of the body. 16 And if the ear should say, "Because I am not an eye, I do not belong to the body," that would not make it any less a part of the body. 17 If the whole body were an eye, where would be the sense of hearing? If the whole body were an ear, where would be the sense of smell? 18 But as it is, God arranged the members in the body, each one of them, as he chose. 19 If all were a single member, where would the body be? 20 As it is, there are many parts, yet one body.

Every local church body is made of many members. I also believe that the greater church body in a city is equally made up of various parts of the body that makes a whole. One church may be very strong in their worship ministries; another is known for their ability to reach people of a certain age. One ministry may have a focus on healing and deliverance, another on family. One ministry may center all of their outreach on the homeless in the city; another may focus more on missions abroad like starting schools and digging wells. One church may rock your face off with their worship style; another has all acoustic worship using mostly hymns. All of these are beautiful expressions of THE BODY of Christ. There's just no way that any one church can do everything that needs to be done by the body. That's why we have each other. The many churches in town are not competition; they are comrades in the battle we have to win the soul of the city!

The problem lies in perception. Much of transfer growth has been the result of the consumer mentality creeping into churches. Many Christians have become church hoppers and shoppers to find the right church that meets all their needs and preferences. They view a local congregation as a country club with perks for the members, not a vital PART OF THE BODY of Christ with a unique calling to be celebrated not scrutinized. A calling that when paired with the other churches in town are meeting the needs of the city and the call of God on HIS BODY to be the church.

Where does that leave you? It leaves you with a great invitation to lock arms with a local church to begin together seeing lives brought to Christ, discipled and cared for. It leaves you with an opportunity to embrace a church knowing that we won't meet every need or preference that you have. We are not a one stop shop. We are not a mall. We are a ministry moving in the areas that God has uniquely gifted us to accomplish. We are so glad you are here and know God will both minister to you and through you as you link up. If this isn't the perfect place for you, just know it's because there are no perfect places. No place that can meet every desire and preference. On the other hand, if this is where God is calling you to link arms, then it is the perfect place to call home.

MAKING CHURCH TRANSITION EASIER FOR CHILDREN AND STUDENTS

Making church transition easier on kids and students is important for many different reasons. One being, that any change in the life of a child can have a positive or negative effect, depending on how the process is handled. With that being said, seeking a church family will not be any different.

In day to day life, children are constantly being introduced to new things. Whether it's starting school for the first time, a new activity or sport, learning to swim, going on a first sleepover adventure, or getting up in front of others. The list goes on and on.

The changes in going from a previous church to a new one or starting consistent patterns of Sunday attendance can be a big deal. Sometimes the relocation to a new town or community, attending a newer church with a more kid-friendly environment or possibly helping with a young church plant during those startup years will be the motivation for a new place of worship.

In this chapter we will look at the "whys" of easier transition, and the "how to's" when moving forward. Because every child and student is unique and different from one another, it's important to implement each child's change in a wise and careful way.

When coming into a new church, if walking through those front doors make you a bit uncomfortable, more than likely your child is sensing the very same thing. Kids are not that different in the way that they process change. Not in all cases however. There's always that one kid that will face any social situation squarely in the eye and find immediate joy in making new friends on that first Sunday. Never thinking of those potential first impression obstacles, they plow right through the awkwardness of being new.

For the rest of our kids, the thought of reinvesting and integrating into a new place will take some time. The sooner that you as a parent can assist them and reassure them through the transition, the better. On the other hand, churches that bridge the gap of acceptance and encouragement also look to find creative ways to reach out to their first time students. For example, there's a genuine sense of worth when a kid gets either a card in the mail, a phone call, or is mentioned on a first name basis from a small group leader each week that can take the sting out of being uprooted and planted in a new place. Ministry doesn't stop there though - it's just beginning. When relationships between student and teacher begins to be cultivated over time and is consistently being watered with the truth of God's word, there's a bond that takes place in these kids that will eventually lead them to a deeper faith in Christ. This builds a solid foundation towards their commitment to church that will take them way into their adult years.

Other families during a transition may have their students coming away from a past church having said goodbye to more than just their close friends. The child or student may have stepped away from a meaningful area of ministry that brought opportunities for growth and purpose in their young impressionable life.

For these types of kids, it's vital for them to get reconnected and grow within a church family that not only encourages serving, but one that offers different ways to participate in areas of service from the start. Again, this may not be the case for all kids, but for those that have taken up a cause in the past by bringing change to the world around them, this could be the difference between leaving or staying, connecting or distancing themselves. So how do parents navigate through all of this? By actively seeking out ways the church's kid and youth ministries teach and create environments of servitude. Missions for example, is a great way to engage and tie kids to a bigger picture by offering them short term missions trips, mission based fundraisers, and serving the church's surrounding city through small outreach opportunities. Another great way to offer areas of service to kids is to allow children to make "Welcome" cards in the first time guest bags that are given out to new families. What a great way to engage the quieter members within your student ministries to help out and begin serving like they did before.

Other areas within the four walls may include things like a kids' greeting team, youth worship, or even training older kids to become helpers with smaller kids in classes on Sunday mornings. Truth is, a younger child will look up and gravitate more towards a teen peer before they will a middle-aged leader. We must learn to engage these amazing youth who have a heart to serve. Not waiting until they've become adults, but rather using them now to mentor and impact the younger generation so that their kids will learn to become role models themselves someday.

Stability in a young person's world looks very much like consistency. Most of us can say that at one time or another, we've grown weary in well doing as we look for that perfect church to come along and meet the whole family's needs. It could become a bigger problem than just finding a perfect church to attend when families don't stay consistent, resulting in a slow fade from weekly attendance. This will prove more harmful for a kid's journey to faith in Christ; because without consistency over time, the commitment to Christ will become contingent upon the church being flawless. Much like a marriage, people don't enter in based on perfection, but on love and commitment. Churches will let us down because they house men. Churches will also uplift us because they house Christ. The greatest gift that we can give our children is the gift of commitment to the House of God, even through the storms of humanity.

As we speak to commitment, another great way to stay engaged within the church and to continue moving forward in attendance is by looking for other like-minded families. The sooner you can begin reaching out and connecting with other parents, the easier the transition can be on your little ones. Finding a church that fosters this environment will be easy to point out as they repeatedly offer small groups for families and other similar events. Parenting classes are great on ramps to join and find other parenting friendships. There's something raw and real about doing life together with one another though the good times and bad, knowing you're are not alone on this journey. You won't remember the parenting struggles nearly as much as you will the people who were there during them. We were never meant to travel this road alone. Teaching your children to be challenged and to lean on one another for love and support speaks of your commitment to a parenting community.

A church that is intentional about partnering with parents will most likely have some sort of parenting-type resource wall or kiosk. If it were to be a visible and central location of such resources, you would be encouraged to glean valuable tools to help your journey through self-help books, possibly some aged- appropriate bibles, student devotionals, or any other tools for the purpose of navigating the phases of each child's life. Although church ministries tend to have different core values, most churches put due emphasis on raising a family. The presentation of how this is laid out will differ in every church, the general idea being the same. As mentioned before, churches that offer small groups or parenting classes encourage families to interact and journey forward together. With this type of investment to partner with parents, children will naturally manage through transition easier when these things are thriving in a church's ministry.

Since growth is key to an ongoing relationship with Christ, children should be invited into a participatory faith each and every week. Although an engaging program is what draws our youth, a deeper understanding of who Jesus is will keep them. When a child experiences a safe environment that allows them to ask messy and tough questions that life throws at them, transitions they're facing in life seem more manageable. All throughout childhood, kids process everything. From rules to social media, they need a moral compass and a place to ask questions. Do we want to be a safe church, or a church that looks messy at times trying to mentor kids in understanding the heart of Jesus? Growth might not look as noticeable on the outside, but the roots over time go deeper than what is seen. Icebergs are usually 70% larger under the surface, much like a child's faith over time.

In closing, the goal of an easier transition for children of all ages is to bring consistency and commitment to them as mentioned above. Allowing kids a thriving place to belong and become involved early on is one way we can speak to their purpose and worth in the kingdom. The ongoing partnership with a child's ministry leader and a parent produces strategy as they teach students the truth of God's word, and then offer a safe environment to ask the sometimes tough questions of faith. Finally, knowing that God created us to do life together, finding a community that gives insight and challenges one another through the easy and difficult phases of parenting is vital. More is done best together.

GETTING BACK TO WORSHIP

"Worship has been misunderstood as something that arises from a feeling which 'comes upon you,' but it is vital that we understand that it is rooted in a conscious act of the will, to serve and obey the Lord Jesus Christ."—Graham Kendrick

Let's be honest. The reason we choose to not worship is because we don't feel like it. In truth, why would we? Life is complicated! It's dirty, filled with immorality, deceit, pain, frustration, deadlines, and schedules that never end. Why would I wake up on any given morning with the thought, "I should get up and go sing songs with a bunch of people because, MAN I feel like it!"

But that's not how we view most other important disciplines in our life, is it? Going to work, exercising, chores around the house, etc... We do these things because we have to, and if we don't there are real world consequences. In all honesty, if we were rich, with some sort of miraculous genetic disposition that finds us in perfect health and fitness no matter how many meals we eat at Dunkin Donuts, and the maid did all the chores, we would do none of these things!! But that's not our life and we do see the value in living a life of discipline that results in our benefit, so we carry on.

And therein lies the rub. We fail to recognize the negative effects that ignoring worship has in our life and rob ourselves of the positive life change that God desires to guide us toward.

We allow worship to become a selfishly motivated nonessential "extra," rooted in preference and availability rather than a disciplined response to God's commandment to be worshiped. (Deuteronomy 6:13)

When exploring the topic of worship, there are 4 things that we must address:

Worship is not a song set list.

Music is fantastic and created for the expressed purpose of connecting our soul to God's.

God saw music and worship as such a priority that he even created an Arc Angel to be in charge of it. Lucifer, created as the Arc Angel over worship, stood in such awe of the power of worship that he plotted to take some for himself. This resulted in his expulsion from heaven along with all his followers to a place we now call Hell.

His continued obsession is wrapped up in taking worship away from God, and one of his most crafty tools just happens to be his specialty...music. Through music we emote and relate in incredibly intimate ways. Back in the day when mix-tapes were a thing, I would create them not by titles, or artists, but by mood. Feeling chill? Give me some Blind Melon and Phish. Needing pumped before a game? Welcome to the Jungle and anything from Marky Mark. I've now exposed you to the unholy preferences of my youth, but you get the point. There's a jam for every mood! Music has that ability to connect with us in a way few things can and take us to places unexplored.

Worship can be powerful in this way because when the worship team picks that one song that was played at youth camp, we get lit! Perhaps that song that really connects with my "deep place" is played and I can finally "enter in".

On the other side of the same thought, however, lies something rather unintended and we begin to see Lucifer's hand in action. Sentiments like, "I don't like the style of that worship, the harmonies are getting lost in the mix and it ruins the song, or it's just too bright or too dark in that room for worship."

All of the sudden we have taken the worship from God and placed it firmly on preference. God is not praised and the enemy has won. Worship is not a set list performed by musicians for our emotional benefit. It's a humbling of ourselves and lifting up of our Lord on high. It's a sacrificial (let that word sink in) act that is meant to bring honor to a great God. Not because He has been great to us this week, but because He is God and worthy of our praise.

Worship is not about us, our preference, or our availability. It is completely about God.

Worship is not emotionally motivated.

I am the father of three incredible sons. One of my chief responsibilities is to guide them from a place of feral emotional outbursts to measured maturity. If you have spent any time around children, you know that they are an emotionally wild bunch. Every decision and action revolves around and is ruled by their current emotional state.

As adults, we can clearly see there is a lot of maturing needed before this person can take care of himself or herself. So, what do we do? We take away options until they have matured to the point of self-discipline. Bed times, brushing teeth, eating balanced meals, going to school, etc. These and more are actions that as an adult we accept and practice without being told to because we have matured to a place of self-discipline.

Maturity lies in the mental (not emotional) decision to live a disciplined life. This may sound harsh, but God is our father, not our baby sitter. He will not force us to pray, study the Word, or worship. He gives us the freedom to make the mature decision to practice these spiritual disciplines. But we have to get to the point where we realize that we cannot rely on our emotional state to dictate when or if we will worship.

Can worship be emotional? Yes. Are there emotions that can encourage me to worship? Yes. But if I wait for the right mixture of emotional stew before I praise, I am completely missing the point. I have once again made worship about me. To the contrary, we have been instructed to worship in EVERY emotion! (1 Thess. 5:16-18) Worship is not the celebration of good times that God may have been involved in, it's an intentional devoted time of expressing honor to the creator of the universe in good times and bad. It's a priority that is protected.

Worship can happen in isolation, but is meant to be expressed corporately.

Jesus is absolutely to be sought out and worshipped in all manner of moments and times of day. Some of my most intimate times with Christ have occurred during personal moments of worship with just my guitar and His presence. All the prophets of the bible spent personal devotional time with God in study and praise, in fact that's where the majority of the book of Psalms comes from. The intimate worship between man and God can be a powerful and transformative thing, but it was never meant to be the "end all".

In Hebrews 10, Paul is speaking to a group of people who had been through some incredibly tough times together and had made it out the other side. They did this by encouraging each other and holding on to the truth of who Jesus is and the promises He had made. When one would waver, as a community they would lift up the one and make him whole. Now, on the back side of their tribulation, things are good. There is less of a reason to "fight the good fight". The dire physical, emotional, and spiritual needs for a "holding fast" to the God who will get us through seem to be non-existent. The result is a group of believers who no longer meet and are quickly losing touch with the Christ who has meant so much.

In verses 24-25, Paul is famously quoted as saying:

"24 And let us consider how we may spur one another on toward love and good deeds, 25 not giving up meeting together, as some are in the habit of doing, but encouraging one another— and all the more as you see the Day approaching."

In other words... We don't just need God and each other when times are bad - we need this fellowship constantly and consistently!

When we gather together, we "fill the well" if you will for when things get dry. We make the connections with people whom (now that we have worshipped with) we know we can rely on to lift us up when we are low. When we cooperate in a community, we position ourselves to be used as a spiritual intercessor for those around us. By gathering together, we publicly declare the greatness of God and experience a sense of unity in Him that we can never experience alone.

Paul is warning all of us to not fall into the trap of thinking that Church and corporate worship is just a spiritual emergency room to be visited when calamity strikes. It is in fact our hedge of protection from and within those very moments.

What's in it for me though?

There are times when nothing makes sense. Times when life has thrown you impossible curveballs for the past few innings, and you are left in a fog of questions, fears, and doubts.

King David found himself in the very same emotional state time after time. He says in Psalm 73:13

"Surely in vain I have kept my heart pure and have washed my hands in innocence. 14 All day long I have been afflicted, and every morning brings new punishments." But then the clarity that only God can bring comes to him in verse 16, "When I tried to understand all this, it troubled me deeply 17 till I entered the sanctuary of God; then I understood their final destiny."

There are times when we can sit and ponder all day long in vain to no avail. Then, we set ourselves and our issues aside to give God the praise he forever deserves, and he is able to speak to a mind that is finally focused on Him.

What's in it for us?

The presence of God.

GETTING BACK TO SERVING

So, you've read this book about how to move forward after being church hurt and now you're on the final chapter about serving. Congratulations! But be warned that starting to serve again is not the cherry on top of your church healing sundae. Beginning to serve again is a vital part of your healing process. Serving your local church acts less like the cherry and more like the hot fudge poured over top. It runs between every scoop of ice cream, every banana, every sprinkle...you can continue this analogy with whatever extra toppings you would like. Serving weaves through all of our hurts and pulls us back into community. It redirects us away from our fears and back to an anticipation to what Christ can do through us.

As you make the choice to serve again we want you to remember - or maybe to know for the first time - that serving is not just checking off your to-do list. This is not community service. These are not hours added to your resume to broaden your horizons. Serving is God's invitation to us to be part of something Holy. He invites us to do the same thing that He did while He was here on earth - to serve. By accepting this invitation, we express Jesus to others in a way that allows them to see Him in us. To see the Jesus that is both sacrificial and consistent.

Why does He want this for us? Honestly, as Christ followers serving is not a request that He makes of us but rather a command that He gives to us. Not because Christ needs more minions following Him around, but because He knows the power that it brings to us as individuals. When you find the place that God is calling you to serve you will experience fulfillment, satisfaction and joy in a way that you won't experience otherwise. So here are 3 quick things that we want you to know as you answer the call that God has on your life to begin serving again.

It's OK to rest.

This particular point may not be a popular one in our world today. We live in a society where if someone asks you "How are things going?" and you don't answer "Busy." then they may look at you funny. "Busy" has become the new default, and while there's nothing wrong with having a full schedule we have to be willing to recognize rest as a healthy necessity. The same thing applies when you are coming off a season of church hurt or burnout. Rest is a vital part of the healing process. As you begin to consistently attend a church again it is important that you do a self-health check of where you are emotionally. Be honest with yourself as you ask, "Have I rested from the things that have caused me pain, burnout, distrust, etc?" If the answer to this question is "no" then that's okay. Your period of rest may not be over yet. And that's okay. What we don't want you to do is to just stop there. Instead, set a physical date and time to do another self-health check. You may have to do two or you may have to do thirteen. Just continue being honest with yourself.

Satan would love nothing more than to discourage you. He wants you to think that you're never going to recover from this and that you'll never get back to fulfilling the serving call God has on your life. Let me encourage you today that you will! Which leads us to our next thought.

It's OK to feel hesitant.

For the last year or so we have had a life size cardboard cut-out of one of our pastors floating around our offices. My coworkers and I use it to startle each other by placing it around corners or behind doors. Recently one of my coworkers put it in the women's bathroom, which has motion activated lights. You can imagine how startled I was when I walked two steps into a dark bathroom and came face to face with the cardboard cut-out right as the lights flashed on. I didn't say any "bad words", but I don't think I said any good words either. We all got a good laugh, but for the next 2 weeks I would slowly open the bathroom door and wait for the sensor to turn the lights on completely before coming around the corner into the bathroom. Understandable, right? That experience had caused me to be hesitant about entering the room again. The same principle applies as you walk back into serving in ministry. You were proceeding through life as normal and then a circumstance occurred that has left you apprehensive about re-entering the room. And that's okay. Hesitation is our natural reaction to prevent ourselves from being hurt again. It's okay to feel hesitant, but it is not okay to feel debilitated. Satan wants to sneak in and give you serving paralysis that debilitates you from moving forward in God's will for your life.

I encourage you to do two things as you navigate your hesitant feelings. The first things is to pick one or two people that you trust to talk through your hesitations with about re-entering the serving arena. These should be people who you trust, people that you feel the freedom to be completely honest with through the process, and people who you know have a healthy lifestyle of serving. We all need people who will keep a protective eye on us, but who will also push us forward if they see that our hesitation is turning towards debilitation. The second thing I would encourage you to do is to have an honest conversation with the pastor or director of volunteers at the church where you re-enter serving. Share your story, to whatever degree you are comfortable, with the individual who you will be working with as you move forward. This will allow the church staff to serve you well as you begin serving others. If you find yourself nervous about sharing your experience, you can write out what you would like to say or even send an email if that is more comfortable for you. This may feel awkward at first, but I promise that it will bring peace to your hesitations!

It's OK to start again.

So now you're rested, you've navigated through your hesitations about re-entering a serving team, and the only things that's left to do is to start again. It seems like it should be easy, but why does your heart still feel that sharp little pain when you think about jumping back into serving? It's the fear of the unknown. The fear that can be summed up into one question we ask ourselves, "Is this going to be the same as before?" This is a valid question for you to ask yourself because you fear that this is going to be another bad experience. Let me reassure you, it will not be the same. These are not the same people as before, and - more importantly - you are not the same as you were before. The Bible teaches us that God takes the hurts and pains from our lives and uses them for our good. Part of that good is helping us learn from our experiences. That may look like helping us learn to say "no" more often, teaching us how to handle conflict with others, or developing discernment within ourselves for our ministry position. God will not let your hurt be in vain. You can trust that while it was never God's plan for you to be hurt, He will not let it hold you back anymore. So, whether you're starting for the first time or maybe for the second, third or fourth time, know that it is okay to start again.

The path to healing is a journey and starting to serve is neither the beginning or the end. It's weaved all throughout. But like I said before, there's something Holy about accepting the invitation that Christ extends to us to serve. And I believe choosing the invitation to serve is also choosing an invitation to healing. Do not choose to forget your past. Instead make the choice to take your past, lay it before God and allow Him to build your future upon it as He heals and restores you.

He has great things for you on this journey.

And He's ready when you are.